# The Pony Express

by Jean Kinney Williams

Content Adviser: Gene Newman, Education Coordinator,
Pony Express Museum, Saint Joseph, Missouri

Reading Adviser: Dr. Linda D. Labbo,
Department of Reading Education,
College of Education, The University of Georgia

**COMPASS POINT BOOKS**

Minneapolis, Minnesota

Compass Point Books
3722 West 50th Street, #115
Minneapolis, MN 55410

Visit Compass Point Books on the Internet at *www.compasspointbooks.com* or e-mail your request
to *custserv@compasspointbooks.com*

Photographs ©: Courtesy Scott's Bluff National Monument, cover, 5; North Wind Picture
Archives, 3 (top), 4, 6, 7, 9, 11, 17, 29; Bettmann/Corbis, 3 (middle & bottom), 8, 22, 28, 37, 41;
Justin Sullivan/Getty Images, 10; Hulton/Archive by Getty Images, 12, 13; Saint Joseph Museum,
Saint Joseph, Missouri, 14, 24, 34; Courtesy Donald Laird, California State Historical Landmarks,
www.calandmarks.com, 16; James L. Amos/Corbis, 18; Corbis, 20; Phil Schermeister/Corbis, 21,
26; Courtesy of the Pony Express Museum, 25; Courtesy of the Pony Express Home Station,
www.xphomestation.com, 30; Stock Montage, 31; Dave G. Houser/Corbis, 33; "Pony Express" by
Frank C. McCarthy, The Greenwich Workshop, Inc., www.greenwichworkshop.com, 35; Nevada
Historical Society, 39; Special Collections, Kansas City Public Library, Kansas City, Missouri, 40.

Editors: E. Russell Primm, Emily J. Dolbear, Sarah E. De Capua, and Catherine Neitge
Photo Researcher: Svetlana Zhurkina
Photo Selector: Linda S. Koutris
Designer/Page Production: Bradfordesign Inc./The Design Lab
Cartographer: XNR Productions, Inc.

**Library of Congress Cataloging-in-Publication Data**

Williams, Jean Kinney.
  Pony express / by Jean Kinney Williams.
    v. cm. — (We the people)
Includes bibliographical references and index.
 Contents: A colorful chapter in the history of the Old West—Getting the mail to California—Two
months to get it ready—The Pony Express is off!—Adventure on the job—Pony Express bows to
telegraph line.
  ISBN 0-7565-0301-9
  1. Pony express—History—Juvenile literature. 2. Postal service—United States—History—
Juvenile literature. 3. West (U.S.)—History—1860–1890—Juvenile literature. [1. Pony express.
  2. West (U.S.)—History—1860–1890.] I. Title. II. We the people (Compass Point Books)
  HE6375.P65 W45 2002
  383'.143'0973—dc21                                    2002002957

# TABLE OF CONTENTS

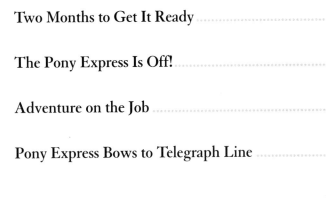

# A Colorful Chapter in the History of the Old West

In one year during the middle of the 1800s, a new state went from being a mildly popular place to a wildly popular one. It was California. The United States won it

*Gold was first discovered at Sutter's Mill in California in 1848.*

from Mexico in 1848, the same year gold was discovered in the Sacramento Valley. In 1849, "gold fever" drew 100,000 new settlers to California from around America and throughout the world.

Getting there was not easy for Americans. Traveling by land meant going over mountains and into deserts. Much of the territory was inhabited by Native Americans who were hostile to white settlers. Traveling by ship meant sailing all the way around South America and back up to

*The Pony Express roughly followed the same route as the Oregon Trail.*

5

California. But these challenges did not deter the forty-niners who dreamed of finding fortunes in California gold.

It was important to people living in the West to keep in touch with family and friends back East. The **telegraph** was the fastest way to communicate, but telegraph wires did not reach all the way across the country yet. As America appeared to be headed for the Civil War (1861–1865), citizens in the West were especially anxious to keep up with the news.

*Western Union workers prepare telegrams in New York.*

**6**

*Wagon drivers threw the mail to post office workers.*

Over time, trails were developed for settlers to follow that led west. There was a southern route and a northern-central route. The government began sending the mail overland on these trails instead of by sea. The U.S. **postmaster general** was a southerner, so he paid the

**7**

*A Pony Express rider on a mail trip*

company that maintained the southern route to carry the mail.

Some businessmen wanted to convince the U.S. government to send mail to California along the northern-central route. In the warmer months, it was much faster than the southern route because it was 800 miles (1,287 kilometers) shorter. And while **stagecoaches** or wagons could not carry mail through the mountains in winter, a single rider on a strong horse could. That is how the Pony Express was born in 1860.

The Pony Express lasted only one and a half years, yet it is one of the most colorful chapters in the history of the American West. Young men, many of them teenagers, rode for hours throughout the day and night in a relay system to carry mail from Missouri to California, a distance of almost 2,000 miles (3,219 km). Even the heat of summer, the snows of winter, and hostile Native Americans could not keep the Pony Express riders from reaching

*An Apache takes aim at a covered wagon.*

9

their stops. Dependable, quick communication from the East played an important part in keeping California in the Union when the Civil War broke out.

"The mail must go through" was the Pony Express motto, and it did, without the comforts of heated or air-conditioned trucks and a lighted highway system. Californians were thrilled to receive mail and news in just ten days. They greatly admired the dedication of the Pony Express riders, whose exciting stories are still remembered.

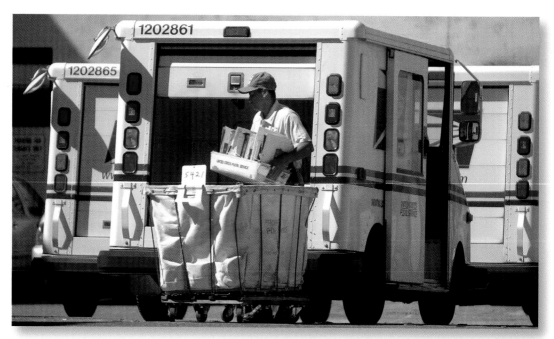

*Today's U.S. Postal Service believes "the mail must go through."*

# GETTING THE MAIL TO CALIFORNIA

When the gold rush swept America in 1849, many settlers heading to California had to pass through Missouri. This made the Midwest a natural gateway to California. On their way there, they bought oxen and other supplies for the long trip.

One concern for new settlers of the West was mail service—it was slow and infrequent. When the government sent mail by boat, the long trip around South America

*Before the Pony Express, mail often had to be hauled by ship around South America to the West Coast.*

*After mail arrived in California it had to be delivered inland to the mining camps.*

and back up the Pacific Ocean to California could take several months. Some ships sailed to what is today Panama in Central America. There the mail was hauled across the **isthmus** to the Pacific Ocean and reloaded on another ship that sailed up to California. Once mail finally arrived at the California coast, much of it still had to travel to miners and settlers living inland. One **entrepreneur**

12

delivered mail from the main post offices to the mining camps. He charged 1 ounce (28 grams) of gold dust per letter and 2 ounces (56 g) for newspapers.

Later in the 1850s, slavery was a huge political issue. It even affected mail delivery. The southern postmaster general, who preferred the mail be carried west

*Slavery and the Civil War both affected mail delivery.*

**13**

along a southern route, hoped this would encourage settlers to move into slave states and territories. That way,
slavery might be expanded into
the southwestern territories.
The huge **freight-
ing** company of
Russell, Majors, and
Waddell, however,
was determined to
get a contract to
carry mail along
the northern-
central route.
William Russell
had an idea for
delivering mail that he
hoped would "build a
worldwide reputation" for
his company, he told his

**14**    *William Russell*

business partners. Russell suggested a relay system between men on horseback. They would travel light, carrying only mail, newspapers, and telegrams. Russell's partners, Alexander Majors and William Waddell, did not think Russell's idea was a good one. Their freighting company, which carried supplies between U.S. Army forts on the Great Plains, was almost **bankrupt.**

Russell hoped a "pony express" would prove that the northern route, called the Central Overland Route, was ideal for mail. He also hoped that their company would be well paid by the government to deliver mail to the West. Late in 1859, Russell, Majors, and Waddell formed the Central Overland California & Pikes Peak Express Company (COCPP), and through that the Pony Express was created.

Russell's son John also worked for the new company. In January 1860, John received a telegram from his father announcing their Pony Express service would begin on April 3. It would take just ten days to travel the central route, an amazing promise for that time. John immediately told newspapers about the upcoming service. "Clear The Track And Let The Pony Come Through," exclaimed a Kansas newspaper headline. The Pony Express was coming!

WESTERN HEADQUARTERS OF RUSSELL, MAJORS, AND WADDELL

THIS WAS THE SITE OF THE WESTERN BUSINESS HEADQUARTERS OF RUSSELL, MAJORS, AND WADDELL --FOUNDERS, OWNERS, AND OPERATORS OF THE PONY EXPRESS, 1860-1861. THE FIRM'S MAIN OFFICE WAS IN LEAVENWORTH, KANSAS. W. W. FINNEY WAS THE WESTERN REPRESENTATIVE IN SAN FRANCISCO.

CALIFORNIA REGISTERED HISTORICAL LANDMARK NO. 696

PLAQUE PLACED BY THE CALIFORNIA STATE PARK COMMISSION IN COOPERATION WITH THE SOCIETY OF CALIFORNIA PIONEERS, APRIL 1, 1960.

*A plaque marks the western headquarters of Russell, Majors, and Waddell.*

# TWO MONTHS TO GET IT READY

The Central Overland company had just sixty-five days to organize the Pony Express. Horses and ponies had to be bought, riders and station keepers hired, and some new stations built. The plan called for riders to carry mail for about 75 miles (121 km) each, stopping every 10 or 15 miles (16 or 24 km) to switch horses at relay stations along the way. At the end of the 75 miles, riders reached the home stations and would finally stop to rest and eat. There, another rider was ready with a fresh horse to begin the next long run.

*Pony Express riders delivered mail using a relay system.*

The Pony Express operation needed about 160 stations, beginning in Saint Joseph, Missouri, and ending in Sacramento, California. This was a distance of nearly 2,000 miles (3,218 km). Some stations already existed, and many more were quickly built. The route roughly followed the Mormon and Oregon–California Trails through modern-day Kansas, Nebraska, Colorado, Wyoming, Utah, Nevada, and California.

*Riders would stop at stations such as this one, which is located on the Oregon Trail in Kansas.*

Approximately 400 horses were bought, which was an expensive investment. Some of them were wiry western mustangs, accustomed to the hot desert climate. Some of the horses were Kentucky Thoroughbreds, which were bred for speed. Horses had to be able to run 12 or 13 miles (19 or 20 km) without stopping.

Newspapers ran notices advertising the need for "skinny, expert riders willing to risk death daily." Riders would earn $50 to $100 a month, a good wage in those days. Working for the Pony Express could be dangerous. This was especially true in the far West, where Paiute Indians were waging war against the increasing number of travelers going through their homeland. The Pony Express route cut right through Paiute territory. A fast horse was a worthwhile investment if it could outrun an angry band of Paiutes. In fact, that was often how Pony Express riders stayed alive.

Nevertheless, there was no shortage of young men hoping to ride for the Pony Express. About eighty riders

*A Paiute stands armed with a rifle. The Paiutes were often at war with the settlers.*

were needed to keep the Pony Express in motion. Many of those hired were still teenagers. Alexander Majors was very strict about the behavior he expected from his employees. Anyone working for Russell, Majors, and Waddell received a small Bible. Each person had to also sign an oath declaring that he would not use **profane** language or drink alcohol.

Each station had a station keeper and a stock tender who took care of the horses. If the station was also used for stage-coach stops or other travelers, it had several employees and more animals. Many stations, especially in the desert, were lonely and rugged. Often they were not more than a shack or even a large hole dug out of a hillside. Station employees also were expected to maintain high moral standards. Though several were killed during Paiute attacks, they seldom deserted their posts even in dangerous circumstances.

Food, such as bacon, flour, coffee, beans, and pickles, was hauled to all stations. Food and supplies for the horses, and things that would be needed around the station, including matches, needles and thread, tools, candles, buckets,

*A man reads in a Pony Express station in Callao, Utah, surrounded by artifacts from when the station was in use.*

**21**

*The trails leading to the West were the super highways of their day. They carried both
supplies and people to the western territories.*

22

brooms, and tin dishes, were also brought.

The *mochila,* a leather cover that fit over the horse's saddle, was an important piece of equipment specially made for the Pony Express. Each rider needed two mochilas: one to carry mail from east to west, and another to carry mail from west to east. On each of the mochila's four corners were boxlike pockets called cantinas that held the mail. The rider kept the mochila in place with his legs as he rode. When it was time for a fresh horse, the mochila could be slipped off the tired horse and onto the next one in an instant.

The eastern starting point of the Pony Express was kept a secret until March 31, 1860, when the Saint Joseph *Weekly West* newspaper proudly announced that Saint Joseph would be the eastern **terminus.** Mail would cost $5 per half ounce, which was very expensive then. (It later was reduced to $1.) But the mail would arrive in California in ten days! That, too, was unheard of in those days, and excitement about the Pony Express's takeoff was growing.

23

# THE PONY EXPRESS IS OFF!

Because the Pony Express charged so much money to deliver a letter, its operators promised the fastest delivery possible. Riders had strict schedules to keep, no matter what the weather or circumstances. That schedule faced its first test before the Pony Express even started.

On the afternoon of April 3, 1860, a crowd gathered in Saint Joseph to see Johnny Fry take off on the first Pony Express run. At 5 P.M., he was supposed to head for the Missouri River,

*Johnny Fry was the first Pony Express rider.*

cross it by ferry while on horseback, then gallop west to the next station at Cottonwood Springs in the Kansas Territory. Fry could not leave, however, until he had the mail. A messenger from the Central Overland company was supposed to be bringing mail gathered in Washington, D.C., New York, and Detroit. He missed a train connection from Detroit to Missouri, however, and was two hours late.

Back in Saint Joseph, townspeople threw quite a

*Johnny Fry leaves Saint Joseph, Missouri, on the first Pony Express ride.*

**25**

*Pony Express riders carried mailbags like this one.*

celebration for Fry's takeoff. Downtown buildings were
gaily decorated, a brass band played, and a bay mare was
walked through the crowd to warm up for her dash to

26

Cottonwood Springs. But still, there was no mail. The horse had to be returned to her stall because bored onlookers were pulling hairs from her tail for souvenirs.

Finally, the crowd cheered when they heard a whistle announce the arrival of the train. Company officials took the letters from the messenger and packed them in the mochila. In a speech, Alexander Majors predicted that soon a "tireless iron horse"—a train—would carry the mail cross-country. For now, however, the Pony Express was the best way.

At 7:15 P.M., Fry swung the mochila onto the horse and sped off as the crowd whooped and hollered and a cannon blasted. Across the country, the people of San Francisco enjoyed their own celebration as the first eastbound Pony Express rider, James Randall, boarded a boat, the *Antelope,* with another mochila of mail. The *Antelope* would sail to Sacramento, where the mochila would begin its journey east with Billy Hamilton.

Hamilton passed on the mochila to Warren Upson.

Upson spent his first ride trying to make a trail through deep snow on his uphill climb in the **Sierra Nevada**. He finished his challenging run, as did all those first riders.

28

*San Francisco residents welcome a Pony Express rider in 1860.*

Fry and other westbound riders even managed to make up for the two-hour delay from Saint Joseph. Celebrations rang out again in Missouri and California when Pony Express riders delivered the first mail in the promised time of ten days. Newspapers trumpeted the achievement and carried news stories that arrived by Pony Express.

*Warren Upson's first ride included snowy trails through the Sierra Nevada.*

# ADVENTURE ON THE JOB

Robert "Pony Bob" Haslam rode one of the most dangerous portions of the Pony Express, in western Nevada. Paiute Indians had declared war on settlers who cut through their homeland on their route to California. Some Pony Express stations were attacked, and station keepers were killed. For three weeks in 1860, the Pony Express had to shut down so it could rebuild stations.

*"Pony Bob" Haslam was one of the most famous riders for the Pony Express.*

Haslam was on his Pony Express run in early May 1860. He arrived at one station and found that all the horses were being used for an attack on the Paiutes. He watered and fed his tired horse, and they continued on. When he reached

30

Buckland's station 75 miles (121 km) later, the next rider was afraid to venture outside the station and refused to leave. Haslam changed horses and rode on. When he finally arrived at Smith Creek station, he had ridden 190 miles (306 km) straight. After a few hours' rest, he went all the way back to Friday's station, where he started. He rode 380 miles (611 km) in thirty-six hours, a Pony Express record. There were other courageous riders, too.

*An Indian attack on a Pony Express rider*

Rider Jim Moore also performed a heroic run. He was resting at Midway station in Nebraska when a west-bound rider arrived with important government messages that needed to get to California. Moore rode 140 miles (225 km) to Julesburg, where an eastbound rider had equally important messages for the U.S. government from California. The station's regular rider had been killed the day before. So Moore, after a ten-minute rest, rode back to Midway, covering 280 miles (451 km) in fourteen hours, forty-six minutes.

Another rider, Melville Baughn, had his horse stolen by a horse thief at Fort Kearny in Nebraska. Baughn set out after the thief, recovered his horse, returned to the station for the mochila, and took off on his scheduled ride. When another rider was crossing the deep and swift Platte River in Nebraska on horseback, the current pulled the horse out from under the rider, who grabbed the mochila and swam for shore. Though the horse was rescued from the river, the rider used a horse belonging to someone onshore to finish his run. Many riders were injured by Indian arrows. One such rider, nicknamed Bronco Charlie, finished a run with an arrow through his hand.

The most famous rider was William Cody. His family settled in the Kansas Territory. He was an expert rider and an expert shot at age fourteen when he was hired by the Pony Express. Later in the 1860s, he earned the nickname

*Melville Baughn's horse was stolen at Fort Kearny.*

"Buffalo Bill" because he hunted buffalo to feed crews laying train tracks for the cross-country railroads. His "Wild West Show," featuring Native Americans, cowboys, buffalo, and horses, became a hit and was performed throughout America and in Europe.

*"Buffalo Bill" Cody as a teenager*

Pony Express riders did not wear uniforms. They usually dressed in buckskin shirts, regular trousers, boots, and a hat. The only guns they carried for protection were revolvers. Rifles were considered too heavy and might slow down the horses.

The dedication of the riders was remarkable. President Lincoln's inaugural address was delivered to California just seven days after it was made. In eighteen

34

*A famous painting by Frank McCarthy of the Pony Express*

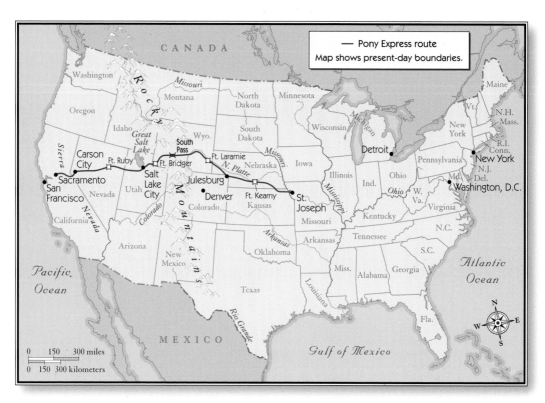

*A map showing the route of the Pony Express*

months of Pony Express service, riders traveled 650,000 miles (1,046,071 km) under sometimes nearly impossible circumstances. Only one rider was killed while on duty, but other riders and station keepers were killed by Native Americans while off duty. Altogether about 200 riders worked for the Pony Express. They were true heroes of the American West.

# PONY EXPRESS BOWS TO TELEGRAPH LINE

On October 24, 1861, telegraph lines finally reached across the continent. Messages could be sent from one end of the country to the other instantly. That put the Pony Express

*A Pony Express rider waves to telegraph workers as he races by.*

**37**

out of business. Even without the telegraph, however, the Pony Express would have struggled to continue.

Even though it was fast and efficient, it did not make enough money. Russell, Majors, and Waddell spent $700,000 to get it started and keep it running, but in eighteen months it only made $500,000. They received small government mail contracts, but that did not provide enough money. Employees of the Central Overland company (or COCPP) nicknamed it "Clean Out of Cash & Poor Pay."

Though the Pony Express helped maintain important contact with the West before and during the Civil War, the government provided it with little help other than the contracts. When the Paiute War shut down the Pony Express for three weeks in 1860, the Central Overland company spent $75,000 to repair the stations and replace horses that had been run off by the angry Native Americans.

Californians were very disappointed when the Pony Express ceased to operate. The California legislature tried to convince the federal government to continue to fund it. By that time, however, the government was devoting its money and attention to the Civil War.

William Russell, Alexander Majors, and William Waddell, who once lived in mansions and owned one of the biggest companies in the Midwest, always seemed to have money problems after the Pony Express shut down. Years later, "Buffalo Bill" Cody was in Denver and ran across Majors.

*Paiute chief Numaga urged his tribe to make peace with white settlers, but raids on the Pony Express continued.*

**39**

Majors lived in a shack and was writing about his life, including the days of the Pony Express. Cody, by then a famous show-man, helped Majors get his story published.

When the Pony Express quit running late in 1861, its story was overshadowed by some-thing much bigger—the country was divided by the

*Alexander Majors*

Civil War. Interest in the remarkable **feats** of the Pony Express was sparked once again early in the 1900s.

40

*Bronco Charlie Miller told stories of his days as a Pony Express rider to Boy Scouts in 1935.*

Former Pony Express riders began telling audiences about their exciting adventures of crossing flooded streams, riding through blinding blizzards, and trying to outride Indians' arrows. Today, their stories are as exciting as ever.

**41**

# GLOSSARY

**bankrupt**—unable to pay debts

**entrepreneur**—a person who begins his or her own business

**feats**—outstanding achievements

**freighting**—the transporting of large amounts of goods

**isthmus**—a narrow strip of land that has water on both sides and connects two larger sections of land

**postmaster general**—the head of the government's postal, or mail delivery, system

**profane**—not showing respect for traditional or religious values

**Sierra Nevada**—a mountain range in east-central California

**stagecoaches**—horse-drawn passenger and mail coaches running on a regular schedule with stops

**terminus**—one of two ends of the Pony Express line

**telegraph**—a system for sending messages over long distances using a code of electrical signals sent by wire or radio

# DID YOU KNOW?

- In 1845, it took six months for a message from President James Polk to get to Americans living in California, when it was still a part of Mexico.

- Because it was so expensive to send mail on the Pony Express, people wrote letters on very thin tissue paper to save money.

- Only fragments of the actual Pony Express trail still exist, so historians have to guess as to the exact route. Some portions of the trail have become dirt roads on private ranches.

- The National Park Service is developing an auto tour route between some portions of the Pony Express route and stations that still exist as historic landmarks.

- The National Pony Express Association holds a reenactment of the Pony Express run every June.

- Bronco Charlie, whose real name was Julius M. Miller, was only eleven years old when he was a Pony Express rider. At age sixty-four, he became one of the oldest soldiers in the Canadian army when he joined to fight in World War I (1914–1918). The American army wouldn't take him because of his age. He died at age 105.

# IMPORTANT DATES

## Timeline

| | |
|---|---|
| **1844** | In May, Samuel F. B. Morse successfully tests the telegraph. |
| **1857** | In September, John Butterfield is granted a contract by the postmaster general to carry mail to California. |
| **1860** | On March 31, the Saint Joseph, Missouri, newspaper announces that the Pony Express would head westward. |
| **1860** | On April 3, the Pony Express takes off from Saint Joseph, with Johnny Fry carrying the first westbound mochila, and from San Francisco, where eastbound rider James Randall and his horse took a boat to Sacramento. |
| **1860** | In May and June, the Pony Express closes down for three weeks after the Paiute War. |
| **1861** | On October 24, telegraph lines were completed cross-country; within a few days, the Pony Express stopped running. |

# IMPORTANT PEOPLE

## JOHNNY FRY

**(1840 –1863)**, *the first westbound Pony Express rider. He was killed while serving in the Union army during the Civil War.*

## ALEXANDER MAJORS

**(1814–1900)**, *began his freighting career by selling supplies to the Pottawatomie Indian tribe that lived on a nearby reservation. He became a partner in Russell, Majors, and Waddell.*

## WILLIAM RUSSELL

**(1812–1872)**, *a partner in Russell, Majors, and Waddell, a huge freighting company that transported supplies across the Great Plains.*

## WILLIAM BRADFORD WADDELL

**(1807–1872)**, *grew up in Kentucky but moved to western Missouri while in his thirties. He became a partner in Russell, Majors, and Waddell.*

# WANT TO KNOW MORE?

## At the Library

Brandt, Betty. *Special Delivery.* Minneapolis: Carolrhoda Books, 1998.

Harness, Cheryl. *They're Off! The Story of the Pony Express.*
New York: Simon & Schuster, 1996.

## On the Web

**The Pony Express Museum**

*http://www.ponyexpress.org*

For Pony Express history, including riders and stations,
as well as a virtual tour of the museum

**Saint Joseph Museum**

*http://www.stjosephmuseum.org*

For information on the history, route,
and riders of the Pony Express

## Through the Mail

**The Pony Express National Memorial**

P.O. Box 244

Saint Joseph, MO 64502

For information and museum publications about
the Pony Express route and riders

# On the Road

**The Pony Express National Historic Trust**

National Park Service

Longs Trail Office

324 South State Street, Suite 250

Salt Lake City, UT 84145

801/539-4093

To visit sites along the trail, which passes through Missouri, Kansas,

Nebraska, Colorado, Wyoming, Utah, Nevada, and California

# INDEX

## About the Author

Jean Kinney Williams lives and writes in Cincinnati, Ohio. Her nonfiction books for children include *Matthew Henson: Polar Adventurer* and a series of books about American religions. She is also the author of *African-Americans in the Colonies.*